Read & Understand

ENGLISH COMPREHENSION

Shab

A BEGINNERS' SERIES

BOOK 2

priority PUBLICATIONS

Published by Priority Publications
info@dspublishers.com

11th Impression 2022

9788180221194

Printed & Bound by : Sanjeev Offset Printer, Delhi - 39

₹ 199

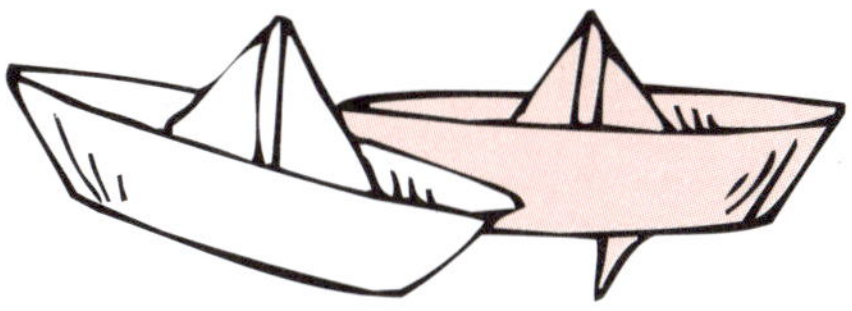

Contents

HOW I SPEND A DAY

My name is Joe. I am six years old. I get up in the morning and brush my teeth. After taking my bath, I wear clean clothes. My mother gives me breakfast.

I go to school in the school bus. I read and write in the school. I come back home in the evening. I play for some time and then do my homework. I take my dinner at seven o'clock and go to bed.

Write True (T) or False (F):

1) I do not go to school. ( )

2) I brush my teeth. ( )

3) I do not wear clean clothes. ( )

4) I go to school in the train. ( )

5) I do my homework. ( )

6) I get up in the afternoon. ( )

7) I read and write in the school. ( )

8) I take my lunch at seven o'clock. ( )

Circle the correct spelling:

1. (a) brush (b) brash
2. (a) clohtes (b) clothes
3. (a) skool (b) school
4. (a) breakfast (b) brekfast
5. (a) homwork (b) homework
6. (a) afternoon (b) aftarnoon

A VISIT TO THE LIBRARY

My sister and I love to read. One day, our mother took us to the library. People were sitting and reading. Our mother told us not to make any noise. We took some comic books. Our

mother gave her library card to the librarian. We collected the books and returned home.

Fill in the blanks:

1) One day, our mother took us to the ______________.

2) We took some comic _________.

3) Our mother told us not to make any _____________.

4) We ____________ the books and returned home.

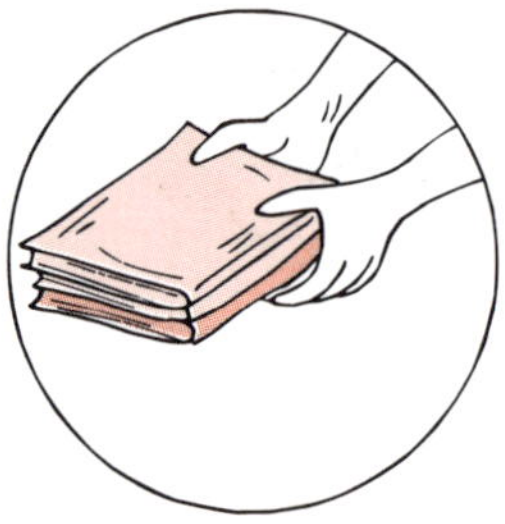

Rearrange the jumbled letters and write the words correctly:

1) stingit

____

2) bilrray

____

3) plepoe

____

4) radineg

____

5) collctede

____

6) nedretur

____

TREE

A tree has many branches. It has got a strong trunk. The trunk is brown in colour. The leaves are green.

Some trees have flowers and fruits. Birds sit on the branches and eat the fruits.

Trees are useful to us in many ways. On hot days, people sit under the shade of the tree to take rest.

Write True (T) or False (F):

1) A tree has no branches. ( )

2) The leaves are blue. ( )

3) Some trees have fruits and flowers. ( )

4) Birds eat the leaves. ( )

5) People sit under the shade. ( )

6) The trunk is brown in colour. ( )

7) Trees are not useful to us. ( )

Complete the paragraph:

A tree has got a _______ trunk. The _______ is brown in colour. The _______ are green. Some trees have _______ and fruits. _______ sit on the branches and eat the _______. Trees are _______ to us in many ways.

MY SISTER

I have a younger sister. Her name is Susan. She is very cute. When she sees me, she smiles. My sister cries when she is hungry. Whenever she tries to stand up, she falls down. I play with my sister.

Tick (✓) the correct option:

1. I have a
a) younger sister. ☐
b) older sister. ☐

2. She is
a) very dull. ☐
b) very cute. ☐

3. I play with
a) my neighbour. ☐
b) my sister. ☐

PICNIC

Last Sunday, my father took us to a lakeside on a picnic. It was a beautiful place. My sister and I played games for some time. We also went for a boat ride. We saw a lot of fish in the lake. Our mother had packed sandwiches, cookies, and orange juice. She spread a mat on the ground and laid out the food. After spending some time near the lake, we went home.

Choose the correct option and fill in the blanks:

1) My sister and I went for a ____________.

Train ride | Boat ride

2) We saw a lot of ____________ in the lake.

Fish | Tortoise

3) Our mother had packed sandwiches, cookies and ____________.

Apple Juice | Orange Juice

MILLY THE KITTEN

Sandra loves cats. She has a kitten at home. Its name is Milly. One day, when Sandra had gone to school, Milly slowly came out of the house and went to the garden. It tried to climb a small tree. Suddenly, the branch broke and Milly fell down. It cried loudly. Sandra's mother came out running and saw Milly lying on the ground. She gently picked Milly up and took it home. She gave the kitten some milk. Sandra came back from school and cuddled her pet.

Match the following:

1) Milly is a	a) climb a tree
2) The branch	b) loudly
3) Milly cried	c) broke
4) It tried to	d) kitten
5) Sandra's mother	e) some milk
6) She gave the kitten	f) came out

Label the pictures choosing the words from the box:

____

____

Climbing
Milly
Branch
Milk

____

____

MY DOG

My dog's name is Judy. Her hair is grey. She has a bushy tail. Judy is a beautiful dog. She has three puppies. They are black.

The puppies are very cute. They take only milk. Wherever Judy goes, the puppies follow her. Judy is very happy with her small family.

Rearrange the jumbled words and fill in the correct answer:

1) Judy is a beautiful __________.

(a) ttoories  (b) dgo 

2) Her hair is ____________.

(a) hiwte (b) regy

3) Judy has three ___________.

(a) piepups (b) tenkits

4) The puppies are _________________.

(a) clabk (b) wnbro

5) The puppies take only_____________ .

(a) kiml 

(b) tewar 

THE RAIN

Yesterday, there were dark clouds in the sky. My mother said, "It is going to rain." This morning, there was very heavy rain. There was water all around the house. We made paper boats and floated them in the water. My friends had come and we all played in the rain water. We liked to get wet. When my mother called us, we went inside and changed our clothes.

Match the following:

1) My mother said,

2) We went inside

3) We liked to

4) There were dark clouds

5) We made

a) paper boats

b) get wet

c) in the sky

d) and changed our clothes

e) “It is going to rain.”

Complete the paragraph:

There were dark ____________ 

in the sky. It rained heavily. We made

________________________  and

floated them in the water. I liked to get

______________  in the rain.

A VISIT TO THE ZOO

Yesterday, our teachers took us to the zoo. We went by our school bus. We were delighted to see a huge lion and a tiger. The gorilla was sitting on a swing. When he saw us, he stretched his hands to us, asking for food. Our teacher had told us not to feed the animals. Two boys sat on the elephant and had a ride. All of us sang songs and had a lot of fun.

Colour the correct option:

1) We went to the zoo by......

Train

School Bus

Car

2) Our ...... took us to the zoo.

Parents

Friends

Teachers

3) The Gorilla was sitting on a ....

Cot

Chair

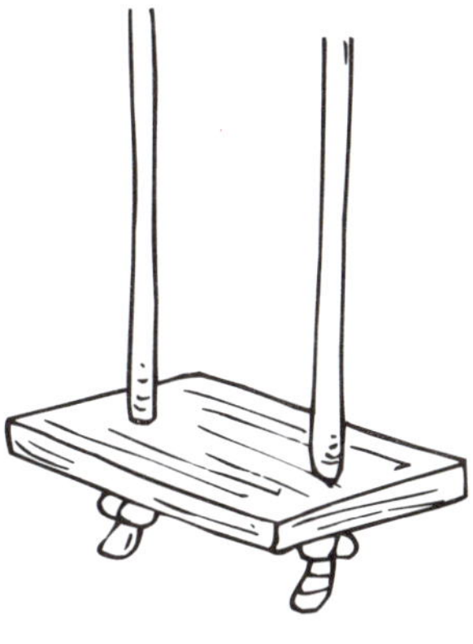

Swing

THE ELEPHANT

I am an elephant. I have a very huge body. My eyes are very small and my tail is short. I have a long trunk. I use my trunk for drinking water. I also like to play in the water. I like banana and bamboo. The man who looks after me is called a mahout. I love children. I carry them on my back and give them a ride. You can see me in the zoo.

Fill in the correct answer:

1) I have a _____________ body.

(a) small  (b) huge 

2) My eyes are _____________.

(a) big (b) small

3) The man who looks after me is called a ___________.

(a) mahout 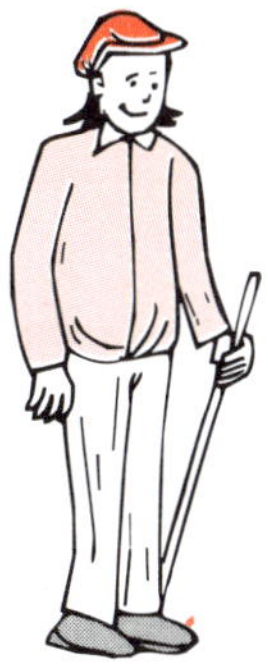 (b) driver 

4) You can see me in the ______________.

(a) zoo (b) playground

5) I use my trunk for __________.

(a) eating 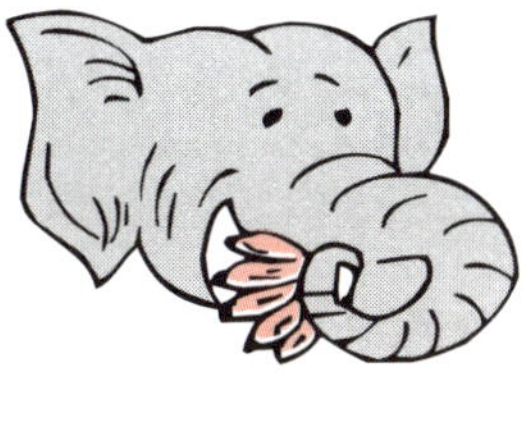 (b) drinking water 

THE CATS AND THE JACKAL

Two cats, Molly and Polly, were great friends. One day, they saw a piece of pizza lying on the roadside. Molly said, "I saw it first. It's mine!" Polly said, "No, its mine!" They started fighting.

A clever jackal saw them and said, "Please don't fight, dear cats. I'll solve your dispute. Both of you close your eyes and count up to five." Molly and Polly closed their eyes and started counting. And when they opened their eyes, they could find neither the jackal nor the pizza! The jackal had run away with the pizza.

Match the following:

1) Molly and Polly
2) They saw a
3) They started
4) A clever jackal
5) The jackal wanted to

a) piece of pizza
b) eat the pizza
c) were friends
d) fighting
e) saw them

Label the pictures choosing the words from the box:

Molly and Polly	The clever jackal
A piece of pizza	The cats fighting

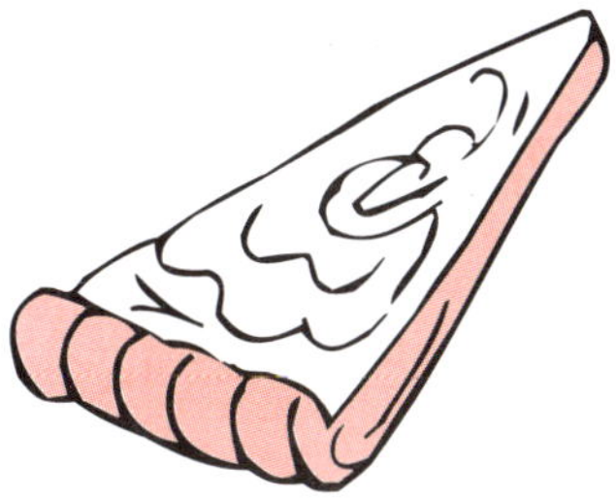

____

____

____

____

GAMES

My brother plays cricket. He and his friends go to a playground to play the game. Sometimes I go with them and watch them play. I don't play cricket. I am small and the bat is heavy. I play 'hide and seek' with my friends.

Write True (T) or False (F):

1) My brother plays tennis.

True ☐ False ☐

2) He and his friends play at home.

True ☐ False ☐

3) I play cricket.

True ☐ False ☐

4) I watch them play.

True ☐ False ☐

PUSSY CAT

Pussy cat, Pussy cat,
Where have you been?
I have been to London
To look at the queen.

Pussy cat, Pussy cat,
What did you there?
I frightened a little mouse
Under the chair.

Choose the correct word from the box and fill in the blanks:

a)	queen	b)	London
c)	chair	d)	mouse
e)	cat	f)	what

1) To look at the __________ .

2) Pussy ______, where have you been?

3) Under the __________ .

4) I have been to ________.

5) ______ did you there?

6) I frightened a little _______.

COLOUR THE OBJECTS

Red

Blue

Green

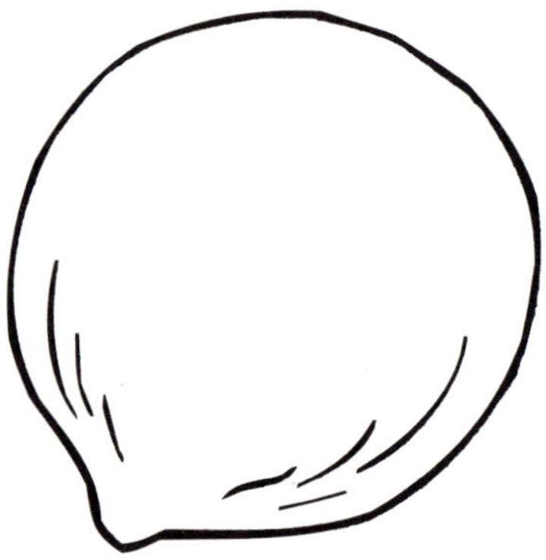

Yellow

Grey

Pink

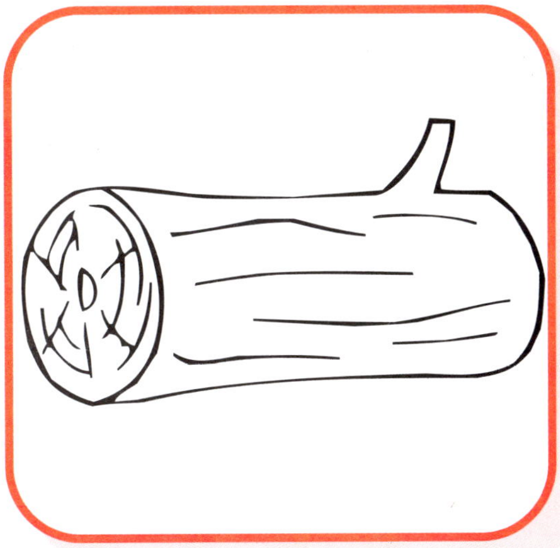

Brown

Purple

THE POSTMAN

The postman brings us letters and cards. He collects the letters and cards from the post office.

Every morning, my father waits for the postman and asks him, "Any letters for me?" Sometimes, the postman brings letters and sometimes he says, "No letters, sir." Our postman wears a brown uniform. I like our postman because he brings lovely birthday cards for me on my birthday.

Fill in the blanks:

1) The postman brings us
_________ and _________.

2) My father waits for the ____________.

3) Our postman wears a brown
______________.

4) He brings birthday cards for me on
my ______________.

5) He collects the letters
from the ______________.

THERE WAS AN OLD WOMAN

There was an old woman
Who lived in a shoe.
She had so many children
She didn't know what to do.

She gave them some broth
Without any bread;
Then whipped them all soundly
And put them to bed.

Match the following:

1) She gave them — a) children

2) She had so many — b) lived in a shoe

3) The old woman — c) soundly

4) She whipped them — d) what to do

5) She didn't know — e) some broth

Label the pictures choosing the words from the box:

broth	bread
shoe	children

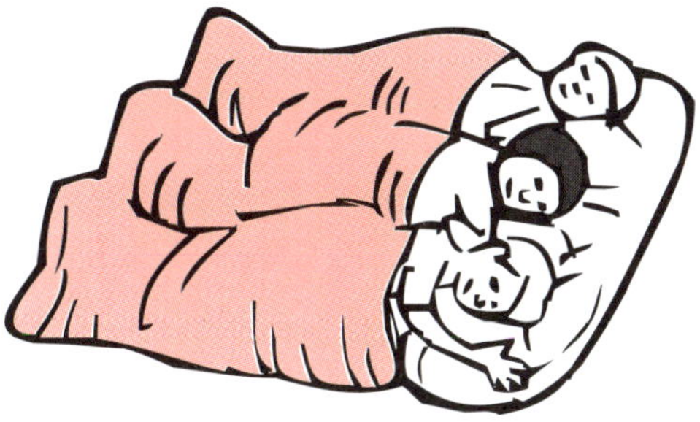

____

____

____

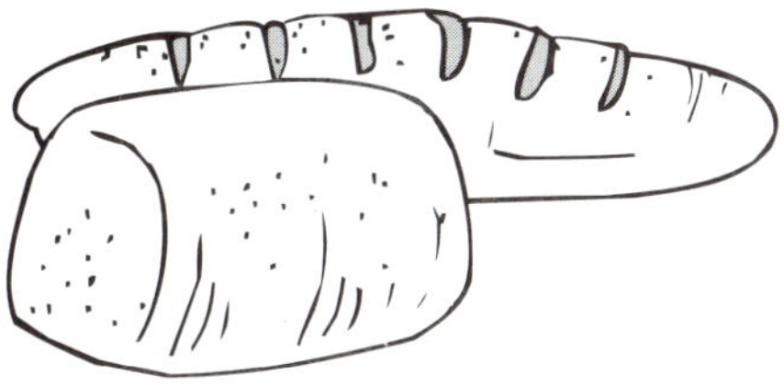

____

ONE, TWO, THREE, FOUR, FIVE

One, two, three, four, five,
Once I caught a fish alive,
Six, seven, eight, nine, ten,
Then I let it go again;

Why did you let it go?
Because it bit my finger so,
Which finger did it bite?
The little finger on the right.

Complete the paragraph:

Why did ____ let it go?

Because it ______ my

_____ so. Which finger

did it ____? The ______

finger on the ______.

Tick (✓) the correct option:

1. **Five** rhymes with
   a) fish ☐
   b) alive ☐

2. **Bite** rhymes with
   a) right ☐
   b) finger ☐

3. **Go** rhymes with
   a) did ☐
   b) so ☐

FROGS

Frogs live both in water and on land. They lay their eggs in a pond. After a few days, the baby frogs, called tadpoles, hatch out of the eggs. The tadpoles have small tails. Their tails help them to swim in the water.

The tadpoles grow up into adult frogs. Frogs eat insects and worms. They leap on to rocks and big stones and catch insects. The frogs catch the insects with their tongue. They croak during rains.

Strike out (✗) the incorrect option:

1)

frogs / stones

4)

insects / rocks

2)

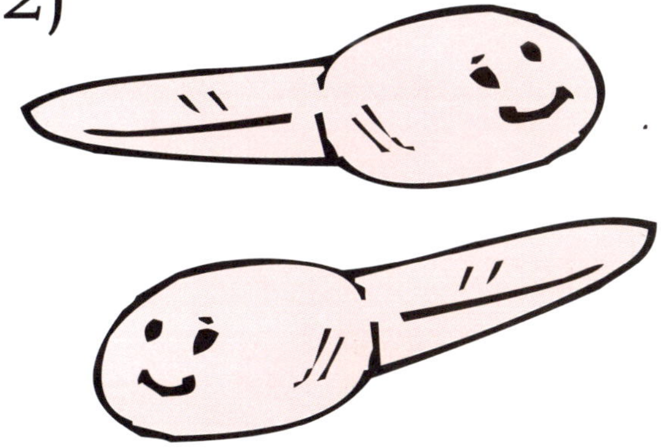

worms / tadpoles

5)

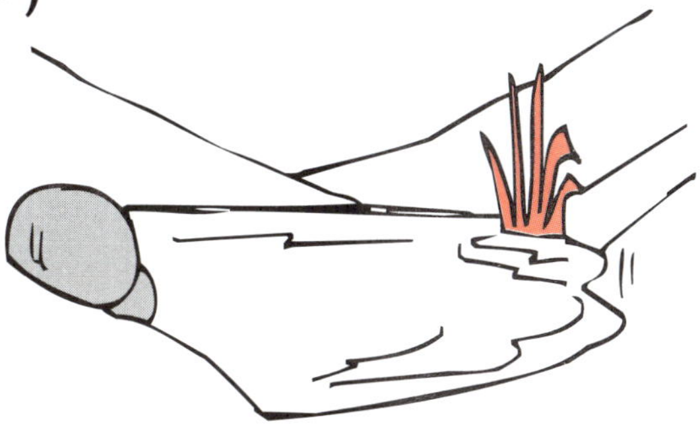

wall / pond

3)

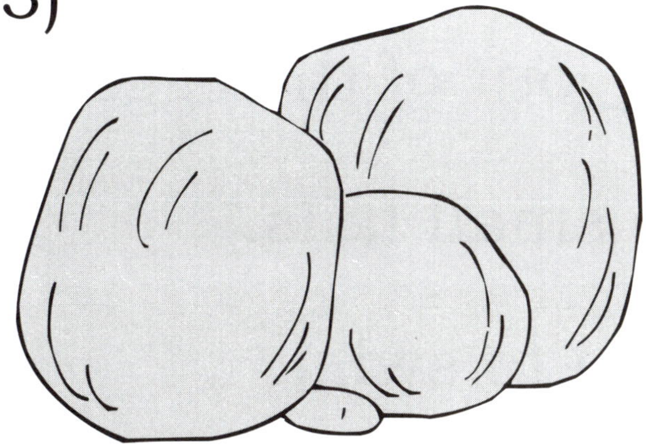

rocks / rains

6)

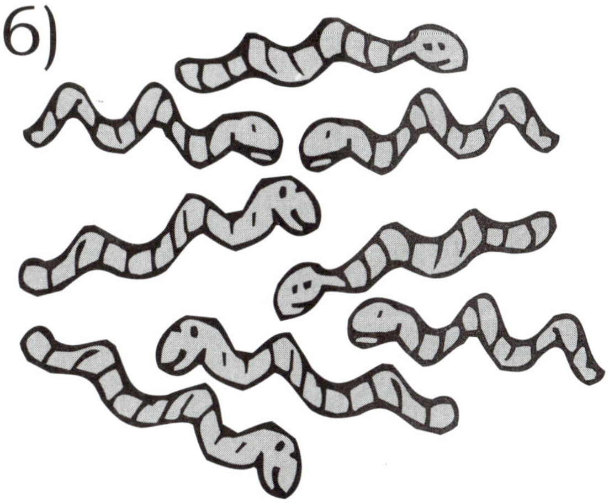

water / worms

Write True (T) or False (F):

1) Frogs live only in water. ( )

2) The baby frogs are called cubs. ( )

3) The tadpoles have small tails. ( )

4) Frogs eat insects and worms. ( )

5) The tadpoles never grow up. ( )

6) The frogs catch the insects. ( )

7) They sleep during rains. ( )

Fill in the blanks:

1) Frogs live both in ______ and on ______.

2) They lay their ______ in a pond.

3) The baby frogs _______out of the eggs.

4) The ___________ have small tails.

5) Their ______ help them to swim.

6) Frogs eat _______ and _________.

MY BEST FRIEND

My best friend's name is Harry. Harry and I study in the same school. We go to school and come back home together. We share our lunch in the afternoon.

Harry and I never fight. We always help each other. I love Harry because he is a very nice boy.

Match the following:

1) Harry and I study
2) We share
3) We always help
4) I love Harry because

a) he is a very nice boy.
b) each other.
c) in the same school.
d) our lunch.

DAVID AND HIS FAMILY

David is six years old. He is doing his homework.

His mother is washing the clothes.

His brother is flying a kite in the garden.

His father is reading the newspaper.

His sister is playing with a doll.

Rearrange the jumbled words and fill in the correct answer:

1) David is ____________ his homework.
(a) ndoig (b) raesing

2) His mother is ______________ clothes.
(a) ingsew (b) hingwas

3) His brother is ______________ a kite.
(a) inflyg (b) ingrunn

4) His father is ____________ the newspaper.
(a) dingrea (b) witingr

5) His sister is ________________ with a doll.
(a) cbingom (b) pinglay

THE CAT AND THE MICE

Ten little mice sat down to spin.
Pussy passed by, and she peeped in.

"What are you doing, my jolly ten?"
"Weaving coats for gentlemen."

"Shall I come and cut your threads?"
"Oh, no, Miss Pussy, you'll bite off
our heads."

Match the text with the pictures to complete the sentences:

1) Ten little mice sat down to......

2) Shall I come and cut your......

3) Weaving ...... for gentlemen.

4) Pussy passed by, and she......

peeped in

spin

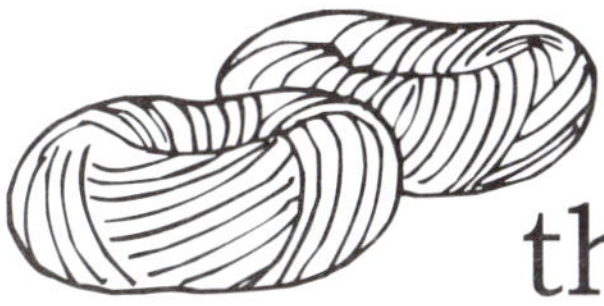

threads

coats

Arrange the lines in the correct order:

1) "Weaving coats for gentlemen." ☐

2) "What are you doing, my jolly ten?" ☐

3) Ten little mice sat down to spin. ☐

4) Pussy passed by, and she peeped in. ☐

MY TEACHER

My teacher's name is Miss Susan. She teaches English. She also teaches us rhymes. When we sing, she also sings along with us. She writes on the blackboard.

When she enters the classroom, we all get up and say, "Good Morning, Miss Susan!" We say "Thank you, Miss Susan" when she leaves the classroom. We all love Miss Susan very much.

Circle the correct spelling:

1. (a) taecher (b) teacher
2. (a) Englihs (b) English
3. (a) rhymes (b) ryhmes
4. (a) blakcbaord (b) blackboard
5. (a) clasroom (b) classroom
6. (a) morning (b) mornign
7. (a) laeves (b) leaves
8. (a) writse (b) writes

Label the pictures choosing the words from the triangle:

blackboard
teacher
book

____

____

____

MY TOY TRAIN

My grandfather gave me a toy train for my birthday. It runs on rails. When it starts, it gives out a whistle and goes "chuk, chuk, chuk" on the rails. It has got an engine. I cannot see the driver because he sits inside the engine. All my friends came to see my train. I let them play with the train. My mother always tells me that I must share my toys with my friends.

Match the following:

1) All my friends came to see	a) with the train
2) I let them play	e) whistle
3) It gives out a	c) driver
4) I cannot see the	b) engine
5) The train has got an	d) my train

Complete the sentences:

1. I have a ________________.

2. It runs on ________________.

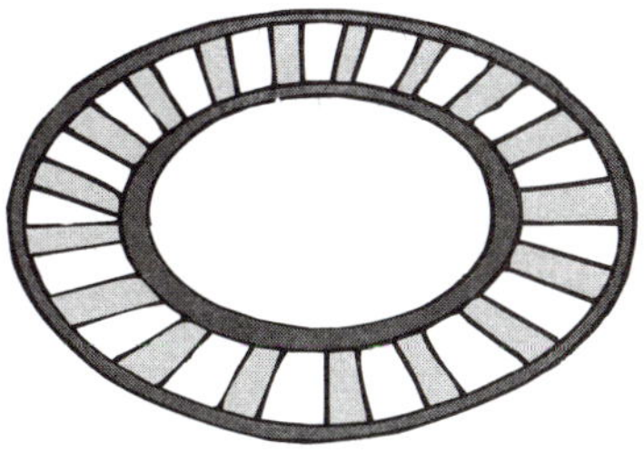

3. It gives out a ________________.

4. It has got an ________________.

THE WISE CROW

It was a very hot day. A crow was thirsty and wanted to drink some water. It searched for water everywhere but could not find any. It flew into a garden and saw a pot. There was very little water in the pot and the crow could not reach the water.

Then, it saw some pebbles near the pot.

The crow picked up the pebbles and dropped them one by one into the pot. The water slowly rose up. The wise crow drank the water and flew away.

Choose the words from the box and complete the sentences:

a) everywhere	e) wanted
b) water	f) drink
c) little	g) pebbles
d) find	h) wise

1) The thirsty crow __________ to _________ some water.

2) It searched for water _____________ but could not __________ any.

3) There was very __________ water in the pot.

4) The crow saw some _______________ near the pot.

5) The __________ crow drank the _________.

Arrange the sentences and the pictures in the correct order:

1) It dropped the pebbles into the pot. ☐

2) The wise crow drank the water. ☐

3) A crow was thirsty. ☐

4) It flew into a garden. ☐

☐ 

☐ 

☐ 

☐ 

MY GRANDFATHER

My grandfather lives with us. He wears glasses when he reads newspaper. He carries a walking stick when he walks. I go along with my grandfather when he goes for a walk in the morning. Sometimes, he plays 'hide and seek' with me. One day, he took me and my friend to a circus. He tells me good stories. He often comes to my school and talks to my friends. I love my grandfather very much.

Strike out (✗) the incorrect option:

1) One day, he took me and my friend to a...

(a) Movie

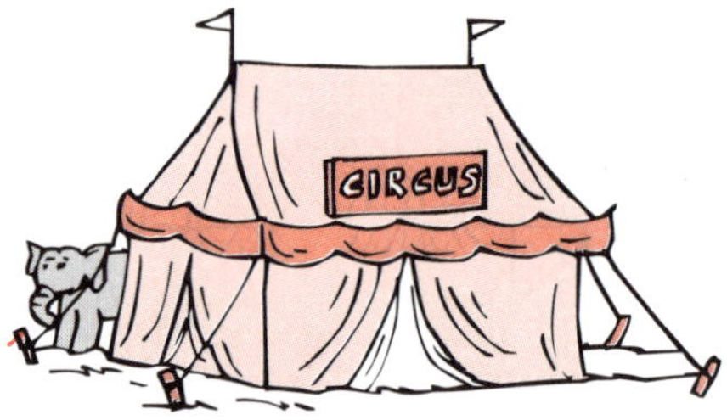

(b) Circus

2) We play...

(a) cricket

(b) hide and seek

3) He carries a...

(a) umbrella

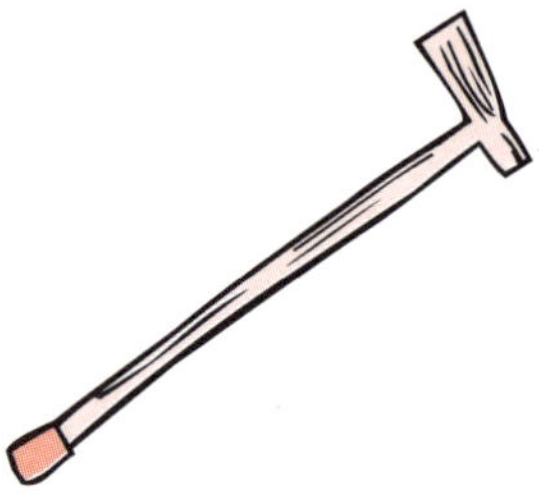

(b) walking stick

4) He talks to my...

(a) teachers

(b) Friends

Rearrange the jumbled words and write the sentences correctly:

1) grandfather my lives us with.

____

2) wears he glasses.

____

3) newspaper reads he.

____

4) walking a stick he carries.

____

5) goes for in the a walk he morning.

____

6) plays and he seek hide me with.

____

ANIMALS AND BIRDS

A **deer** has antlers.
It can run very fast.

An **owl** is a bird
with large eyes.

A **giraffe** has a
long neck.

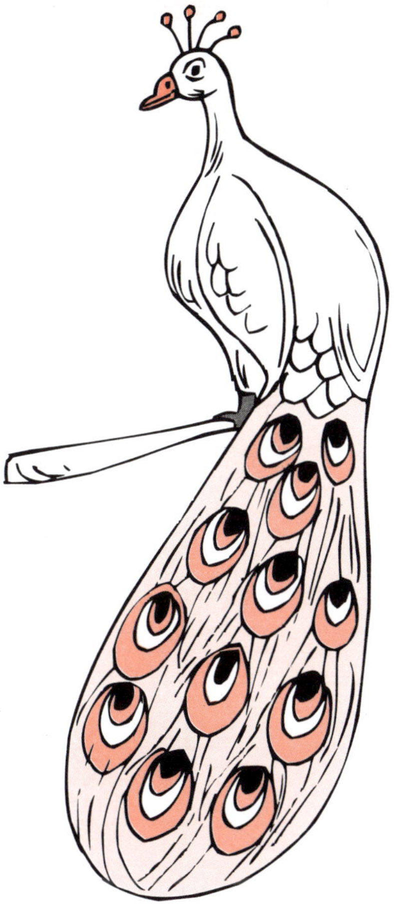

A **peacock** has coloured feathers.

A **duck** loves to swim in the water.

A **zebra** has stripes on its body.

A **crow** is a large, black bird.

A **rabbit** is a small animal. It has long ears.

Fill in the correct answer:

1) A Giraffe has a ______________ neck.
   (a) short (b) long

2) A Rabbit is a ____________ animal.
   (a) small (b) big

3) A peacock has ____________ feathers.
   (a) black (b) coloured

4) An owl has _______________ eyes.
   (a) small (b) large

5) A crow is a large ______________ bird.
   (a) white (b) black

Match the animals and birds with their characteristics:

1) 

2) 

3) 

4) 

5) 

a) A large, black bird.

b) Loves to swim in the water.

c) A small animal with long ears.

d) Has stripes on its body.

e) Has antlers; can run very fast.

MY STUDY ROOM

I always keep my study room clean. I have a table and a chair in my room. I do my homework sitting in my room. I keep all my books and toys in the cupboard. When my friend comes home, I take him to my room. We sit and read storybooks. Every morning, my mother keeps some fresh flowers on my table. I feel very happy when I enter my room and see the fresh flowers.

Choose the correct word from the box and fill in the blanks:

(a) cupboard	(b) table, chair
(c) storybooks	(d) clean

1) I always keep my room ____________.

2) I keep all my toys in the ____________.

3) We sit and read ______________.

4) I have a ______ and a ________ in my room.

Match the following:

1) When my friend comes home	a) sitting in my room.
2) I do my homework	b) when I enter my room.
3) I feel very happy	c) I take him to my room.

WHAT DO THEY SAY?

The dog says BOW-WOW!

The cat says MEOW!

The sheep says BAA-BAA!

The clock says TICK-TOCK!

The hen says CLUCK-CLUCK!

The cock says COCK-A-DOODLE-DO!

Tick (✓) the correct option:

1) The dog says MEOW.

True ☐ False ☐

2) The sheep says BAA-BAA.

True ☐ False ☐

3) The clock says Wee-Wee.

True ☐ False ☐

4) The cat says MEOW.

True ☐ False ☐

5) The hen says BOW-WOW.

True ☐ False ☐

Underline the vowels (a, e, i, o, u):

1) BOW-WOW

2) BAA-BAA

3) CLUCK-CLUCK

4) TICK-TOCK

5) COCK-A-DOODLE-DO

OLD MOTHER HUBBARD

Old Mother Hubbard
Went to the cupboard
To get her poor dog a bone.
But when she got there
The Cupboard was bare
And so the poor dog had none.

Choose the correct letters and complete the word:

1) Moth__ (er, ar, re) 2) b__e (on, no, en)

3) the__ (er, re, ri) 4) ba___ (er, re, ne)

5) Hubb__d (er, ar, re) 6) W__t (en, ne, nt)

A VISIT TO A SHOP

My mother took me to a big shop this morning. She wanted to buy some bread and butter and other things. My mother told me I could take anything I liked. I took two bars of chocolates. My mother said, "Don't eat it now. We have to pay for it." So, I put it along with the other things. She paid the money and we went home. I enjoyed my shopping.

Colour the correct option:

1) My mother took me to a big ...

(a) school

(b) shop

2) I took two bars of...

(a) cakes

(b) chocolates

3) I enjoyed my...

(a) eating

(b) shopping

Fill in the blanks:

1) My mother took me to a ________ shop.

2) She wanted to buy some _________ and ________ and other things.

3) My mother said, “Don't eat it _____. We have to _____ for it.”

4) So, I put it ____________ with the other ___________.

5) She paid the ______ and we went ______.

Rearrange the jumbled letters and write the words correctly:

1) mherot __________

2) mingorn __________

3) wedant __________

4) btteur __________

5) athingny __________

6) chotescola __________

FRUITS

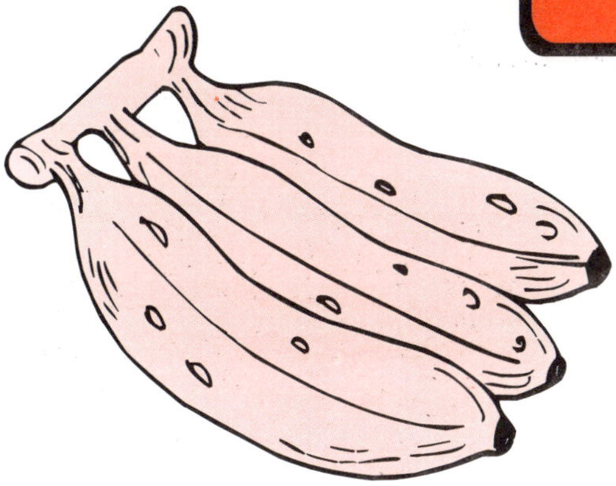

Bananas

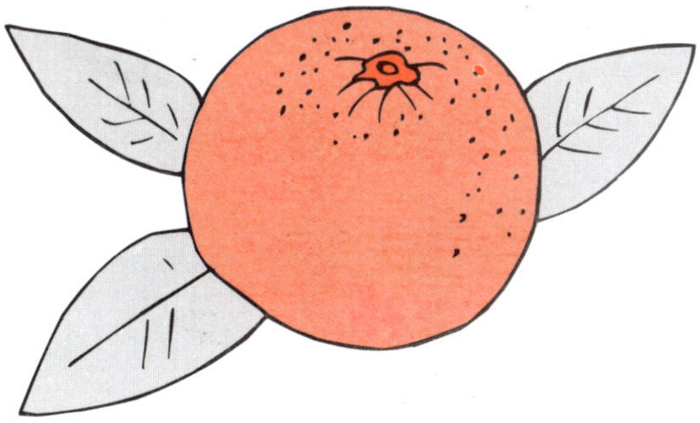

Orange

Apple

Grapes

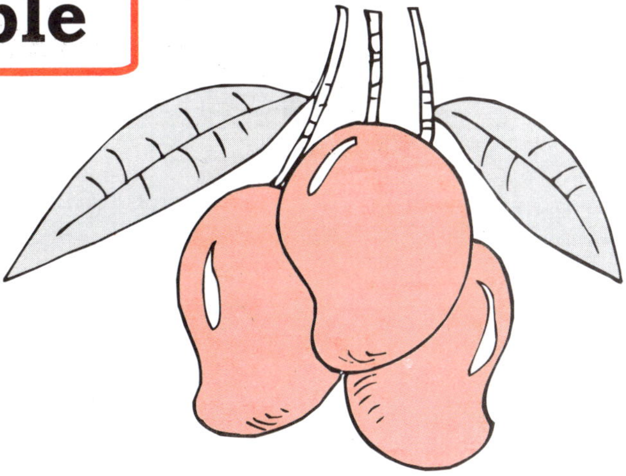

Mangoes

Watermelon

FLOWERS

Rose

Lily

Jasmine

Sunflower

Tulip

Daisy

Tick (✓) the correct option:

1) Apple is a flower.

True ☐ False ☐

2) Mango is a fruit.

True ☐ False ☐

3) Rose is a fruit.

True ☐ False ☐

4) Watermelon is a flower.

True ☐ False ☐

Match the objects with their names:

1) 

2) 

3) 

Lily

Orange

Sunflower

Bananas

Apple

Jasmine

4) 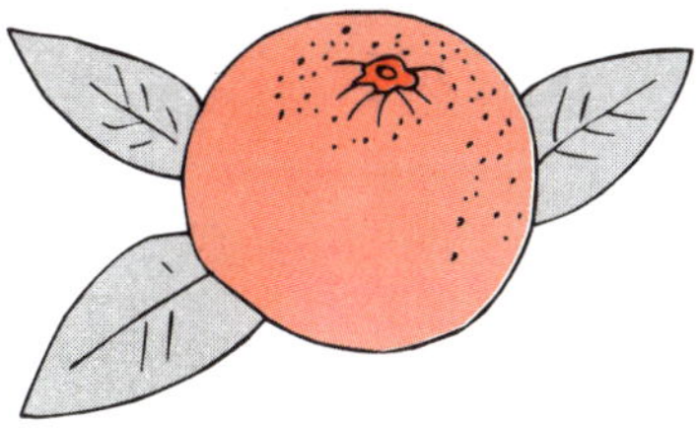

5) 

6) 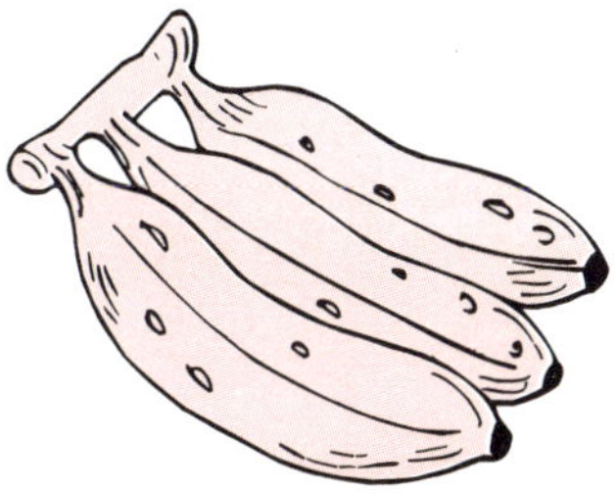

THE DOG AND THE BONE

One day, a hungry dog saw a bone lying on the roadside. Taking the bone in his mouth, he walked on. He reached a small bridge over a stream. While crossing the bridge, he looked down into the water and saw his own image there. The foolish dog thought that it was another dog with a bone. He wanted to get the other bone also. He opened his mouth and barked, "Bow-wow!" As he opened his mouth, the bone fell into the water. The dog felt sad and went away without any bone.

Match the pictures with the text:

1) There was a small bridge over a stream.

2) The dog had a bone in his mouth.

3) The bone fell into the stream.

4) A bone was lying on the roadside.

Circle the correct spelling:

1. (a) bridge (b) brigde
2. (a) imege (b) image
3. (a) reached (b) raeched
4. (a) opend (b) opened
5. (a) straem (b) stream

I AM A BRAVE BOY

One day, while I was playing in the school, I fell down. My knee hit on a stone and was wounded. The wound started bleeding. My teacher came running and carried me inside my classroom. She gently applied some antiseptic cream on the wound and tied a bandage on my knee. It was very painful but I did not cry at all, because I am a brave boy.

Fill in the correct answer:

1) I fell down while __________ in the school.
   a) playing   b) sleeping

2) My __________ hit on a stone.
   a) hand   b) knee

3) My __________ came running.
   a) mother   b) teacher

4) She tied a __________ on my knee.
   a) bandage   b) rope

Underline the articles (a, an, the):

1) I was playing in the school.

2) My knee hit on a stone.

3) The wound started bleeding.

4) The teacher applied an antiseptic cream on the wound and tied a bandage.

5) I am a brave boy.

MY MOTHER'S GARDEN

We have a beautiful garden at home. There are pink roses, lovely jasmines and white lilies in our garden. I help my mother in watering the plants. I love to watch the colourful butterflies and bees flying around. My mother grows vegetables and fruits also. I like potato, cauliflower, carrots and beans. Sometimes, she gives some fruits and vegetables to the neighbours. They thank my mother.

Match the following:

1) I help my mother	a) and fruits also
2) My mother grows vegetables	b) lovely jasmines in our garden
3) I like potato, cauliflower	c) in watering the plants
4) There are pink roses and	d) carrots and beans

Label the pictures choosing the words from the box:

butterflies	flowers
fruits and vegetables	bees

____

____

____

____

INSECTS

Spider:
A small insect with eight legs.

Cockroach:
A large, black and brown insect found in dark places.

Grasshopper:
An insect with long legs.

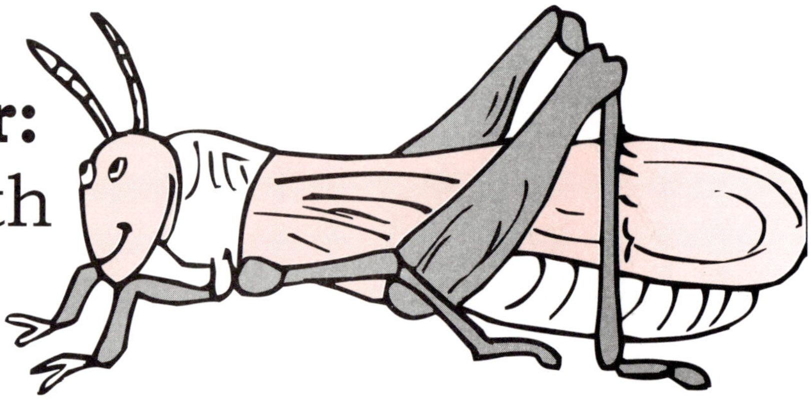

Butterfly:
An insect with beautiful wings.

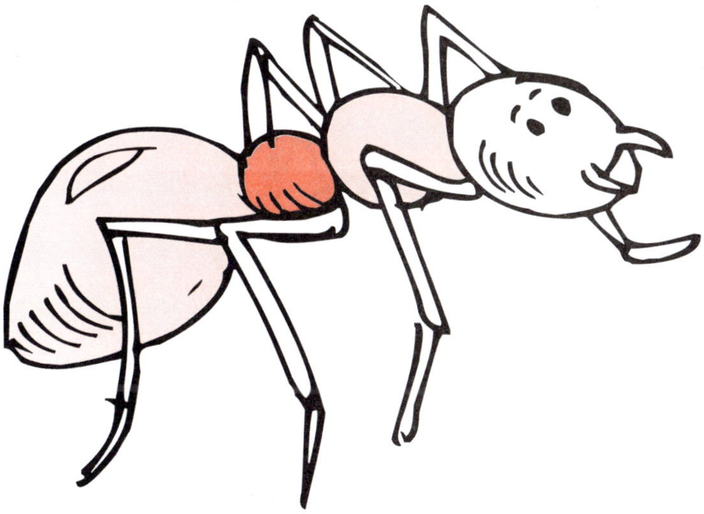

Ant:
An insect which lives in groups.

Bee:
An insect which collects honey.

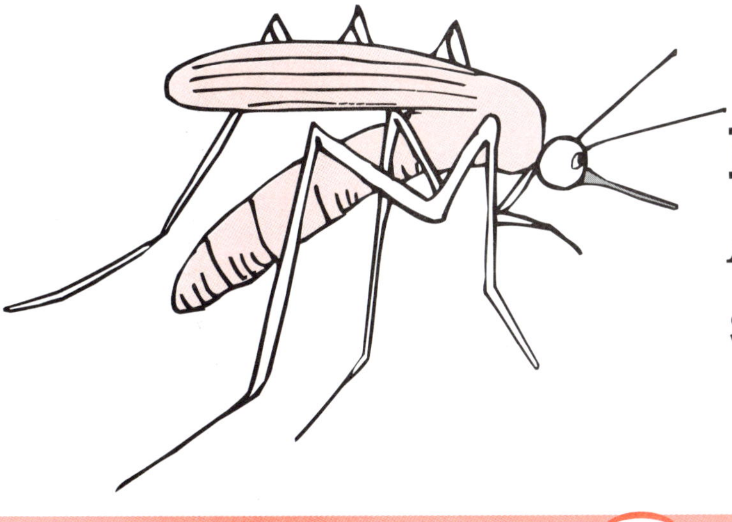

Mosquito:
An insect which sucks blood.

Fill in the correct answer:

1) A spider has ____________ legs.

(a) six (b) eight

2) A butterfly has __________wings.

(a) beautiful (b) white

3) A grasshopper has ______ legs.

(a) long (b) short

4) A mosquito sucks _________.

(a) honey (b) blood

5) A bee collects ____________.

(a) water (b) honey

Match the insects with their names:

1) 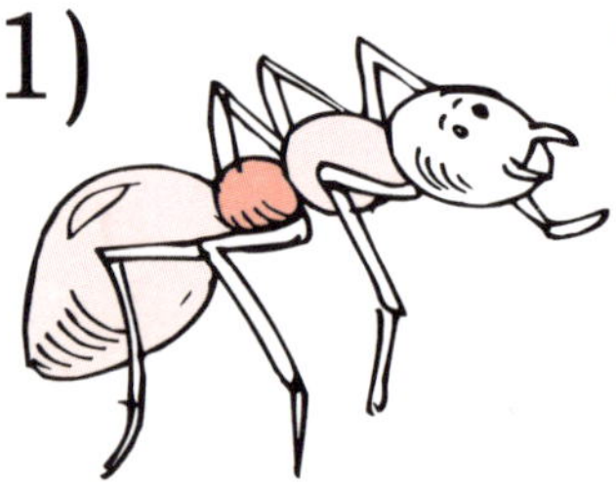

2) 

3) 

4) 

mosquito | spider | bee | ant

ANSWERS

Page 6
Write True (T) or (F):
1) (F) 2) (T) 3) (F) 4) (F) 5) (T) 6) (F) 7) (T) 8) (F)

Circle the correct spelling:
1) (a) 2) (b) 3) (b) 4) (a) 5) (b) 6) (a)

Page 8
Fill in the blanks:
1) library 2) books 3) noise 4) collected

Rearrange the jumbled letters and write the words correctly:
1) sitting 2) library 3) people 4) reading 5) collected 6) returned

Page 10
Write True (T) or False (F):
1) (F) 2) (F) 3) (T) 4) (F) 5) (T) 6) (T) 7) (F)

Complete the paragraph:
strong, brown, leaves, flowers, Birds, fruits, useful

Page11
Tick (✓) the correct option:
1) a 2) b 3) b

Page 13
Choose the correct answer and fill in the blanks:
1) Boat ride 2) Fish 3)Orange Juice

Page15
Match the following:
1) d 2) c 3) b 4) a 5) f 6) e

Label the pictures choosing the words from the box:

Climbing

Milly

Milk

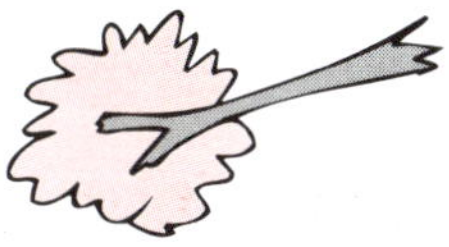
Branch

Page 17
Rearrange the jumbled words and fill in the correct answer:
1) (b) dog 2) (b) grey 3) (a) puppies 4) (a) black 5) (a) milk

Page 19
Match the following:
1) e 2) d 3) b 4) c 5) a

Complete the paragraph:
clouds, paper, wet

Page 21
Colour the correct option:
1) School Bus 2) Teachers 3) Swing

Page 23
Fill in the correct answer:
1) (a) 2 (b) 3) (a) 4) (a) 5) (b)

Page 25
Match the following:
1) c 2) a 3) d 4) e 5) b

Label the pictures choosing the words from the box:

A piece of pizza

Molly and Polly

The clever jackal

The cats fighting

Page 27

Write True (T) or False (F):

1) (F) 2) (F) 3) (F) 4) (T)

Page 29

Choose the correct word from the box and fill in the blanks:

1) a 2) e 3) c 4) b 5) f 6) d

Page 33

Fill in the blanks:

1) letters, cards 2) postman 3) uniform 4) birthday 5) post office

Page 35

Match the following:

1) e 2) a 3) b 4) c 5) d

Label the pictures choosing the words from the box:

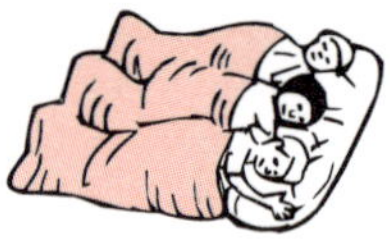
children

broth

shoe

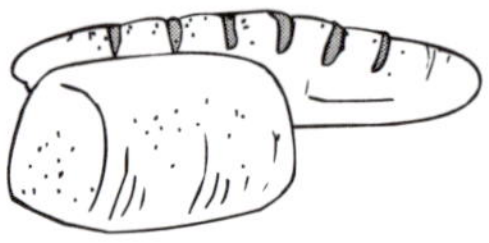
bread

Page 37

complete the paragraph:

I, bit, finger, bite, little, right

Tick (✓)the correct option:

1) b 2) a 3) b

Page 39

Strike out (✗) the incorrect option:

1) stones 2) worms 3) rains 4) rocks 5) wall 6) water

Page 40

Write True (T) or False (F):

1) (F) 2) (F) 3) (T) 4)(T) 5) (F) 6) (T) 7) (F)

Fill in the blanks:

1) water, land 2) eggs 3) hatch 4) tadpoles 5) tails 6) insects, worms

Page 43

Rearrange the jumbled words and fill in the correct answer:

1) (a) doing 2) (b) washing 3) (a) flying 4) (a) reading 5) (b) playing

Page 45

Match the text with the pictures to complete the sentences:

1) Ten little mice sat down to......

2) Shall I come and cut your......

3) Weaving ...... For gentlemen.

4) Pussy passed by, and she......

Page 47
Circle the correct spelling:
1) (b) 2) (b) 3) (a) 4) (b) 5 (b) 6) (a) 7) (b) 8) (b)

Page 49
Match the following:
1) d 2) a 3) e 4) c 5) b

Complete the sentences:
1) toy train 2) rails 3) whistle 4) engine

Page 51
Choose the words from the box and complete the sentences:
1) wanted, drink 2) everywhere, find 3) little 4) pebbles 5) wise, water

Page 52
Arrange sentences and the pictures in the correct order:

1) 3 2) 4 3) 1 4) 2

1

2

3

4

Page54
Strike out(✗) the incorrect option:
1) (a) 2) (a) 3) (a) 4) (a)

Page 55
Re-arrange the jumbled words and write the sentences correctly:
1) My grandfather lives with us. 2) He wears glasses. 3) He reads newspaper.
4) He carries a walking stick. 5) He goes in the morning for a walk.
6) He plays hide and seek with me.

Page58
Fill in the correct answer:
1) (b) 2) (a) 3) (b) 4) (b) 5) (b)

Page 59
Match the animals and the birds with their characteristics:
1) (c) 2) (e) 3) (d) 4) (b) 5) (a)

Page 61
Choose the correct word from the box and fill in the blanks:
1) clean 2) cupboard 3) story books 4) table, chair

Match the following:
1) (c) 2) (a) 3)(b)

Page 64
Tick (✓) the correct option:
1) False 2) True 3) False 4) True 5) False

Underline the vowels (a, e, i, o, u):
1) BOW-WOW 2) BAA-BAA 3) CLUCK-CLUCK 4)COCK-A-DOODLE DO

Page 65
Choose the correct letters and complete the word:
1) mother 2) bone 3) there 4) bare 5) Hubbard 6) went

Page 67
Colour the correct option:
1) (b) 2) (b) 3) (b)

Page 68

Fill in the blanks:

1) big 2) bread, butter 3) now, pay 4) along, things 5) money, home

Re-arrange the jumbled letters and write the words correctly:

1) mother 2) morning 3) wanted 4) butter 5) anything 6) chocolates

Page 71

Tick (✓) the correct option:

1) False 2) True 3) False 4) False

Match the objects with their names:

Sunflower

Lily

Apple

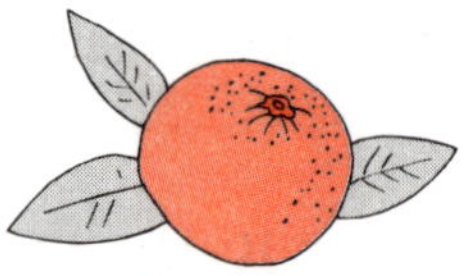
Orange

Jasmine

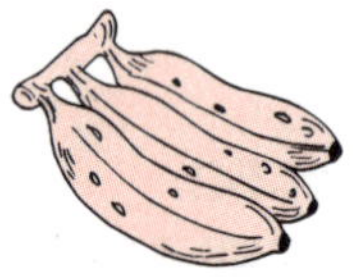
Bananas

Page 73

Match the pictures with the text:

1) There was a small bridge over a stream.

2) The dog had a bone in his mouth.

3) The bone fell into the stream.

4) A bone was lying on the roadside.

Circle the correct spelling:

1) (a) 2) (b) 3) (a) 4) (b) 5) (b)

Page75

Fill in the correct answer:

1) a 2) b 3) b 4) a

Underline the articles (a, an, the):

1) I was playing in the school.
2) My knee hit on a stone.
3) The wound started bleeding.
4) The teacher applied an antiseptic cream on the wound and tied a bandage.
5) I am a brave boy.

Page 77

Match the following:

1) c 2) a 3) d 4) b

Label the pictures choosing the words from the box:

bees

flowers

butterflies

fruits and vegetables

Page 80

Fill in the correct answer:

1) b 2) a 3) a 4) b 5) b

Match the insects with their names:

1) 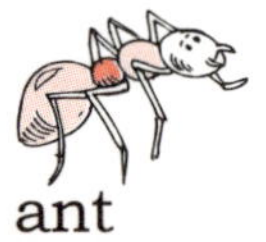
ant

2) 
bee

3) 
mosquito

4) 
spider